Real Estate Investing for Passive Income

*How to Create Passive Income and Financial Well-Being
Through Real Estate Investments*

Table of Contents

Introduction

Congratulations on downloading *Real Estate Investing for Passive Income*. In this book, you will learn how you can obtain financial freedom by taking advantage of the real estate market. Real estate is arguably the best investment that you can make, and skillfully investing can allow you to live the life you have always wanted by freeing yourself from the hustle and bustle of a 9-to-5 job. This means more time for your family, more time for the things you love, and more time to engage in whatever brings you happiness and fulfillment.

Real estate is regarded as such a good investment because the value of real estate naturally rises with economic expansion and inflation. This means that any investment in real estate will likely increase in value over time without any active effort on your part. The other aspect of real estate that makes it such a good investment is that it is an easy source of income. Although real estate is a catch-all term that can include many different types of property, many properties yield income in the form of rent from tenants—hence, not only will your property increase in value over time, but you will also be receiving steady income during the process.

There are other reasons why real estate is such a great investment—most of which we will touch on in greater detail throughout this book. A good real estate investor knows how to use the banking system to their advantage—i.e., getting creative with loans and equity as they acquire more properties. You may be surprised to find how easy it is to build a real estate empire once you have made your first investment in a property or two. The banking system in the United States is certainly not hostile to the investor—and once you have acquired your first property for passive income, it becomes a breeze acquiring more.

Before we delve into a summary of the contents of the book, let's take a moment to talk about passive income. Many analysts believe that passive income—or non-traditional forms of work, in general—is the direction that employment is headed in the future. This means that many Americans are shifting towards non-traditional work hours or multiple sources of income not only to make ends meet but also to increase their net worth and achieve financial freedom. What this means for you is that *now* is the time to get a hand in this trend while you still have the chance to achieve great success.

As more Americans look to ways of getting passive income, including through real estate investing, you may find more competition out there—hence, now is the time to start while the market is still favorable and while there are so many opportunities to invest in.

This is a good time to talk briefly about passive income. What is passive income? Passive income is revenue that is generated for you without a significant investment of time on your part. A quick example of passive income is internet marketing—although real estate is a form of passive income that has been around for much longer.

The goal of this book is to prepare the beginner for a lucrative life in real estate investing. This will require that you gain an understanding of all aspects of the real estate market—from how to go from being a beginner with no experience in the market to understanding how to handle tax issues and invest in more properties. The goal of this book is to give someone with no knowledge or experience in real estate the tools to be able to achieve true financial freedom. Financial freedom means not only the freedom to do what you want because you have the money to do so but also having the free time to be able to live as you choose.

We begin this book by preparing you for your real estate adventure by detailing the American real estate market in 2019. Many readers may know that markets can be subject to upswings and downturns—and the real estate market is no different. The market is linked to factors like interest rates set by the Federal government as well as the global economic picture. Successfully navigating the real estate market requires that you understand where the market has been in the last several years and where it is today. This will be discussed at length in the first chapter.

Chapter 2 is meant to prepare you for real estate investing by discussing some of the important concepts in real estate. The chapter will also lay the groundwork for your investment by discussing such factors as what you need to get started and how big of an investment you should make. The reality is that any investment poses some deal of risk, but one of the great things about real estate investing is that this field generally has lower risks than other business investment options that you have.

The third chapter dives into the subject of passive income and how you can use real estate to generate passive income for yourself. Although many people choose to have passive income while still retaining their full-time jobs, we approach the subject from the standpoint of how you can be so successful at generating passive income to the point that you can leave your job and devote your time to the things that you love to do. Real estate investing can really involve a minimal time commitment, so we discuss the sorts of things that will occupy your time when you decide to pursue this route.

The following chapter deals with leaving your full-time job as well as everything that comes along with that. The real issues with leaving your jobs involve things like taxes, various types of insurance, and all the various financial concerns that come along with not having full-time employment while still having expenses. Timing is always important to pay attention to, so the time when you should quit your job (right away versus waiting a while) will be discussed here.

Finally, we break down all the steps of real estate investing as a form of passive income in the fifth and final chapter. By this point, you will understand all that you need to know about the real estate market, passive income, investing in real estate, and leaving your job. You will be poised to tackle this new adventure, and this chapter will list for you in step-by-step fashion how you can get started in this journey.

We know that you are prepared for your foray into real estate because you took the initiative to download this book. The real estate market is one that anyone can find success in as long as they are equipped with the proper tools. *Real Estate Investing for Passive Income* will provide you with those tools—allowing you to get as much out of this endeavor as you can and live the life that you deserve.

Chapter 1: The Real Estate Market

Interest rates are a topic that many people in the real estate market were talking about in 2018 and are still talking about going into 2019. Interest rates were raised three times by the Government in 2018, a sign of a good economy—but it was also a change that had put real estate investors into a pause. The interest rate should not impact your decision to go into real estate investing, and as you dive into the net two chapters, you will understand why. Rising interest rates are often a sign of a good economy, and the interest rate situation may make it easier for you to nab that property you have been eyeing for a while—but we are jumping the gun a little bit here.

In order to really understand how to handle changes in the market, such as rising interest rates, you need to understand where the market has been and where it looks to be this year. Combine that with an understanding of real estate terms and concepts that you will get in the next chapter, and you will be well on your way to leaving your mark in the real estate world.

Before we embark on our detailed study of the market in 2018 and 2019, let us spend a moment talking about why real estate is a good investment. Although there are a number of reasons why real estate has long been regarded as the best investment you can make, these reasons generally hinge on the basic concept that housing is a basic necessity of life that tends to increase in value over time. This is different from other forms of investment that can change wildly in value due to a number of factors like the stock market or currency trading.

Although the real estate market, too, can be impacted by a number of factors outside the general state of the economy, real estate tends to be a safer bet than other investment options that individuals with capital have the option of investing in. It goes without saying that there is always the possibility that a property may stagnate in value over time or may even fall in value—but in this book, we hope to help you distinguish between those properties that represent a good investment and those that do not.

Because everyone needs housing, there will always be renters on the market looking for a home or apartment to rent. Contrast to this is investing in the restaurant business, for example, which tends to be greatly impacted by the recession. People do not need to eat out, so fine dining at restaurants tends to be one of the first expenses that people chop out of their spending when time gets tough. However, men, women, and families will always need a roof over their heads—hence, there will always be a need for a home to rent or buy.

Real estate values tend to increase gradually over time due to a number of factors including economic expansion, population increase, increased demand, inflation, and many others. This is important to note because some may have heard that the real estate market is "cooling" or is in the process of cooling in 2018 going into 2019. In reality, there has been a drop over the last several years in new home construction, which means that there is actually a relative shortage in the number of available units—thus, property values are likely to increase in the short term.

What this means for you is that despite the sometimes grim picture that you may or may not have heard about the real estate market, it still represents arguably the best investment that you can make with your money. When you also consider that investors in the residential real estate market have a steady income in the form of rent, there are few investments that can compare to residential real estate.

Let us take a moment here to distinguish between real estate investing that you do in the house that you live in versus real estate investing for passive income. Investing in a house is certainly an important investment, perhaps the most important investment that many people will make—however, this is a little different from investing for the purposes of income. This book will teach how to find the right property for you to buy with the goal of generating regular income that you can expand over time by acquiring more property.

On top of that, increases of value in your property also mean increased revenue for you without having to acquire more property. No, we are not suggesting that you become a slum lord who increases the rent without regard to economic factors or the needs of your tenants. We are merely noting that as the GDP increases and the economy grows, the costs of goods and services also increase—and that includes rent. There are laws in most jurisdictions governing when and how you can increase the rent, with the goal being to protect the renter from predator landlords (which we know you have no intention of being).

The Current Market for Real Estate

There tends to be a lot reported on the real estate market in the news, and it is sometimes difficult to know what to believe and what not to believe. The media can sometimes give you a doom-and-gloom sort of picture because they know that this is the best way to get the attention of the viewer—but sometimes, you as a viewer may be left without a clear idea of how to interpret what you have seen and heard. Here, we hope to go over some of the major trends in the market so that you can have an idea of how you may be impacted as a new real estate investor.

The purpose of going over these trends is not to deter you from investing; quite the opposite, in fact. We hope to show you that in spite of the Fed's increase in interest rates throughout 2018, the market still represents a perfect opportunity for a new investor looking to enter for the first time. By exploring these trends, we hope to give you the knowledge to allow you to make the right decision: a decision that is thought out and acquired with a full understanding of where the real estate market is at the present time.

So what were the big trends of 2018 and what direction is the market likely to take in 2018? We already touched on the interest rate situation. As the Fed increased interest rates three times in 2018, this means that anyone looking to get a mortgage is likely to have a higher payment than what they would normally have. What this means for you as an investor is not as clear as it may seem at first, as we will explore later. Yes, it means that your own mortgage payment for a property you invest in may probably be $100 or $200 higher than it might otherwise have been, but it also means that more people are likely to rent rather than buy, which then gives you a stronger market of potential tenants.

Interest rates, however, are only one of several issues that the market displayed in 2018, and which are likely to be important in 2019. Let us summarize them here.

- A general reduction in new housing construction

- A general lack of supply of affordable housing

- Changing economic patterns

- Many renters on the market looking for a unit to rent

- Prior (or possibly more) increases in interest rate

Let us tackle these issues one by one. A general reduction in new housing construction means that there are fewer units being added to the market for buyers to buy. Although new construction numbers have been slowly rising in the last few years, they are being outpaced by population growth and the number of people looking to buy. This has caused an increase in housing values in some places, which makes the picture even murkier. Areas in which houses are valued high because of a lack of available units may straddle the line between a good investment and a bad investment, which we will discuss later.

A lack of supply of affordable housing has been a stable concern in many parts of the country, especially in some urban areas like New York City. A lack of affordable housing is a problem, as it can make it difficult for individuals and families to find housing that fits the funds that they have available. It also means that many people may be looking for affordable rental units, which is its own item on the list of trends. What this means for you is that you can find your niche in this market by successfully being able to match people with the housing their looking for by renting to them at a fair market rate. In short, there is no shortage of people looking for rental units.

Changing economic patterns encompasses several economic trends. Unemployment rates have been dropping, but there also has been a shift towards temporary workers, part-time workers, self-employed, and other non-traditional workers. What this means is that though the economy appears to be doing well right now, it may be subject to rapid changes, as many workers may not actually have steady employment and may be living paycheck to paycheck.

As mentioned above, there are many workers on the market looking for rental units. There are a number of reasons for that. You may already be getting the idea that many of these issues are interrelated. Rising interest rates may cause potential homebuyers to rent rather than buy. A relatively slow rate of new constructions means that housing values may be a little inflated and there may be fewer units to choose from, also tending to push people towards renting. What this means for you is that if you do make the decision of buying to rent or to resell, you actually are poised to do well because of the numbers of people looking to rent.

Finally, the interest rates again. As we hinted at earlier, rising interest generally indicates that the economy is doing well. The Fed tends to raise interest rates when it feels that it needs to curb things a little. Sort of like when OPEC raises oil prices. They generally do that when the market for oil is good, not when it is bad. Again, this means for you that you may be paying a little more on your mortgage, but you should take comfort in knowing that you are entering a market that is still strong.

The Previous Housing Bubble (2007)

Real estate represents a solid investment for those with the capital to invest, although there is always a concern about the housing recession and the housing bubble. The economic picture for the United States is strong. However, it is a good idea to take a look at the housing bubble so that you can be introduced to the idea of how you can protect yourself and your investments.

What is the housing bubble? A bubble is a term for a market that is overpriced and which eventually collapses, leading to foreclosures, bankruptcies, economic downturn, and all of the things that investors (and the Government) worry themselves to death over. Without going into too much detail about the bubble, we can say that it was multifactorial in its causes. The bubble was caused by inflated values in housing, true, but this was related to a global bubble, and to a drop in interest rates in the early 2000s.

The drop in interest rates in 2001 was perhaps one of the biggest factors leading to the housing bubble burst of 2006-2007. A drop in interest rates encouraged borrowing (and lending). This meant that banks and financial institutions oftentimes lent to people who were not actually able to pay, especially in the face of a potential economic downturn and falling housing prices. The long and short of it is that the market was artificially inflated, with many homes being listed for and selling for much more than they were worth. Combine this with the inability of people to actually pay their mortgages, and you can see why this became a problem.

Many of you may be familiar with the term subprime mortgage and subprime lending. A subprime loan is a loan in which the borrower may find it hard to pay back the loan due to poor credit, history of default or missed payment, risk of bankruptcy, or other factors. A reduction in interest rates was closely tied to the subprime lending crisis (or bubble), with the immediate issue being that a large number of borrowers were unable to make their payments, which led to a large number of foreclosures and the bankruptcy of a number of lenders that had made subprime loans.

The takeaway point here is that even if there are the naysayers out there predicting an economic downturn, this is really a different situation than the housing bubble burst of 2007. We are not dealing with unusually low rates of interest or lenders giving loans to riskier borrowers. The current issues in the housing market are the potential for an economic downturn in the future leading to falling housing prices, and whether some real estate markets may be inflated due to a relative shortage of available units.

Making a Good Investment

The last issue to talk about here is that of making a good investment. We still have to delve more deeply into some of the real estate concepts that you should familiarize yourself with in order to make the best investment—but at this point, you should have a general idea that not every real estate investment is a good one. Clearly, purchasing a property that appears to be overpriced based on its location, size, or amenities would represent a poor investment. Although it is typical for some real estate markets to be more expensive than their counterparts in other parts of the country, you will have to get a sense of whether or not a property is overpriced and therefore represents a poor investment.

There are other issues that impact whether or not a property is a good investment. A property is a good investment if it appears to be realistically priced compared to other units in the area and its value is likely to increase over time. A property may also be considered a good investment if it does not require an excessive amount of work at present or in the future in order to rent it or resell it. You may be tempted to buy that house that needs a lot of work because it is so inexpensively-priced, but if you cannot afford all of the work the property will need at the present time than it really is not the best investment.

We can take a moment here to talk about renting versus reselling, which we will go into more detail on later in the book. This book assumes that you are planning to purchase properties with the goal of renting them. We make this assumption, as the rent that is collected from a property is typically more construed as passive income than a property that you are actively repairing in order to resell. Get the difference?

Repairing or flipping a property will require a fair amount of work on your part. That does not mean that you cannot resell it. A property that does not require too much work can be held on to for a certain period and later sold. Indeed, you may decide to do that if you feel that property values in the area are falling or likely to do so in the future. One of the things to keep in mind when buying a property for resell is buying at the right price. You DO NOT want to buy an overpriced property if you are planning on flipping it. You should be wary of buying in overpriced neighborhoods. If you are planning on reselling, make sure that you hone your negotiating skills to bring that price down!

Without inundating you with too much information, this is a good place to summarize what comprises a good investment. In real estate, there is the concept of return. This is essentially what you get back on your investment. In this case, when you purchase a property, the return would be the amount of rent that you get back based on the investment that you made in the property. The monthly rent can be multiplied by 12 to get the return for the year, and then that is calculated as a percentage of your investment. So if you are charging $500 a month in rent, that is $6,000 for the year. If you invested $120,000 in cash in the property, then the return is 5%.

A good investment is one in which you can expect a good rate of return for your investment. Return is only one half of the good investment issue, as the other half is appreciation. Your property should appreciate, or increase, in value over time. You want your investment property to do both. Your property may have a good return in the first year or two, but if you purchased an overpriced property and it eventually falls in value, then we technically would not consider this a good investment. In the next chapter, you will use this information to start investing.

Chapter 2: Investing in the Real Estate Market

Investing in the real estate market is a good idea, as it represents one of the best ways of guaranteeing an appreciation on your investment with minimal risk. Every investment carries with it some risk, but the advantages of investing in real estate are that this risk is kept at a minimum (if you make a good investment), and you can make a good, steady rate of return on your investment with relatively little effort.

How can we define real estate investing? Real estate investing can be defined as acquiring (purchasing) real property for the purpose of making a profit. Property here does not have to be a house, land, or even a condo. Some people choose to invest in what's called Real Estate Investment Trusts (or REITs). These involve several individuals investing in a portfolio of properties that they hold together. Without going into too much detail on trusts here, we can briefly say they have the advantage of being protected from downturns in the market or from problems with a specific property because they are essentially a portfolio of properties deriving returns from multiple sources.

So you are ready to make your investment—but what do you need to know in order to get started? Let us start out by listing clearly all the ways that you can invest in real estate. Many of you may be choosing to invest in real estate by purchasing a house, land, and the like—but there are many ways that you can take your hard-earned cash and turn it into a solid investment. Here, we will list the major ways that a beginning investor can get into the real estate market.

- Purchasing a rental property

- Purchasing and reselling properties (flipping)

- Renting space in a property that you already own

- Investing your capital in a real estate project

- Investing in a real estate investment trust or REIT

Most of you are likely planning to begin your foray into real estate investing by acquiring a rental property. Rental property does not have to be a house or other large property. Indeed, as issues of affordable housing have become more palpable (as we mentioned above), a rental property is frequently a room in a house or a condo. In a legal sense, a condominium is a property that conveys much the same rights as a house. If you purchase a multi-bedroom condo, you can rent out additional bedrooms in the space and collect rent.

Many people choose to invest in real estate by engaging in what is conventionally known as flipping. Flipping involves acquiring a property with the intent of repairing and reselling it. Properties acquired for the purchases of flipping are not intended to be held onto long-term but are rehabbed and resold for a profit. Although flipping cannot exactly be termed "passive" income since you are not collecting rent but are gaining profit by selling the "flipped" property for a higher price, once you have established your initial real estate investment and eventually gain a portfolio, you may choose to involve yourself in flipping.

Flipping often entails a larger investment than merely purchasing a property as there is typically significant repair of the property involved (to increase its resell value), though one of the topics we will discuss here is the different ways that you can fund the purchase of a property. Property purchases do not have to be funded by cash in hand. You may choose to use the equity that you have in an existing property, participate in a government program to get a low down payment rate or another purchasing advantage, or purchase with a partner. There are a number of ways that you can acquire properties with little or no cash.

For many people, their first endeavor into real estate investing is renting a space in a house or property they already own. If you are doing this, you basically are engaging in the business of real estate investment for passive income as you are generating income by renting a space that you own. Although we do not anticipate that you plan on stopping here, if you are already own a property, you do have the option of beginning your first forays into the business here. There are many businesses that you can use to rent your property like Airbnb.

You may choose to begin your investment journey by investing your capital in a large project. There many large projects that are looking for investors, and if you have the capital you may choose to begin your journey here. The advantages here are that this investment would be truly passive as there will be others doing essentially all of the work entailed in generating income. The downside here is that you will have little or no control in the project, but the chances of a return on your investment can often be quite high.

A REIT is almost like a mutual fund as you are investing in companies that have a portfolio of commercial real estate properties from which they derive revenue. This form of investment pays dividends, which is good for those planning retirement, or anyone who is looking for passive income. Again, this is a hands-off form of investment in which all of the work is essentially done by others. There are several ways to get involved in REITs. Many are publicly-traded, making them similar to stocks. You will have to do your homework before you get started, but getting into this venture is quick and easy.

Important Concepts in Real Estate Investing

One of the good things about investing in the real estate market is that it is not difficult to get involved. You can learn as you go, and the concepts that you learn will become more obvious, almost second-nature, as you delve more deeply into the endeavor. It is a good idea to develop a basic familiarity with some of the concepts of real estate that you are likely to be facing. We have already discussed the concepts of appreciation and return, and here are some others that it will help you to know.

Appraisal: The appraisal is the value of the house, aside from what you are actually paying for it. Banks typically require you to have the house appraised before you close. This protects the bank by making sure that they are not providing you with a mortgage for a drastically overpriced property. A bank may deny a mortgage for a specific property based on the appraisal.

Closing Costs: Closing costs refer to the gamut of fees that the buyer will have to pay aside from the down payment of the house. These can run to about five percent of the purchase cost of the home, and they include things like various taxes, fees, and insurance that the law requires when purchasing a home.

Pre-approval Letter: A pre-approval letter is a document from the bank or lender attesting to how much they will lend you for the purchase of the property. This is a good guide as to what you can reasonably expect to purchase.

Fixed Rate Mortgage: This is a loan that has a set interest rate for the duration of the mortgage. A 30-year term of a mortgage is common, though there are other term options. The interest rate does not change over the life of the mortgage.

Adjustable Rate Mortgage: An adjustable rate mortgage has an interest rate that changes over the lifetime of the mortgage. This is an option for people who may want to pay less at the beginning over the mortgage and just pay more in the future—perhaps assuming that they will have a greater income later in the term of the mortgage. This is also a good option for those planning to resell before the higher rate kicks in.

How Big of an Investment Do You Need to Start?

This is an important question that most people considering investing in real estate are likely asking themselves. As you have seen, there are many different ways to get involved in the real estate market in 2019. You do not have to go the traditional route and invest cash in a house, land, or condo. You can invest money in a REIT, rent out a room in your house, et cetera. Most of you will be planning on investing in a new property that you plan on renting, and this section is tailored to that crowd.

The truth is, you can invest any amount that you feel comfortable investing. The market is so varied in the United States that there is no good answer to give you here. What we can say is that you should be conscious of the risks that come with acquiring debt, and this includes debt in the form of a mortgage. There is the possibility that you may not be able to pay the debt back, that you may have an emergency requiring a large outlay of cash, and the like. You should be cautious about investing beyond your means or taking on a debt with a low rate of return (or possibility for depreciation). This would represent a bad investment.

As a general rule, we can say a few things about how much you should invest. First of all, it is a good idea not to invest all of your money. Keep some aside for emergencies, expenses that you will have if you are not working, and the like. If you are planning on reselling the property that you are purchasing, then you need to be especially conscientious about how much you are investing as the costs of repair can easily exceed the down payment you are making on the property.

The other issue here is that you are new to the real estate market. Although participating in this market is not difficult, you do want to give yourself some time to get comfortable. You want to avoid making mistakes. Avoid purchasing a property that appears outside of your budget or too good to be true. Perhaps there's a property for sale in an expensive neighborhood that requires a lot of work. It may seem like a good investment, but can you afford the work it will take to bring it up to the point where you can rent it, or, at the very least, resell it if you have to? Do not take on more than you can chew.

Investing Full-Time Versus Part-Time

This book is for anyone planning on using real estate investing to generate passive income, although it is designed for the person looking to leave their job and perhaps get some much needed free time. Many people that leave their jobs choose to invest all of their free time in real estate as they quickly get hooked by the thrill and excitement of the field. There is certainly nothing wrong with that, but there is a difference between the person lying on the beach sipping margaritas with all their passive income piling up and the person who's busy flipping houses all day.

We will get into this subject more in the fourth chapter—but the reality is that if you are planning on leaving your job, it probably is because you are looking to give yourself a certain lifestyle. If you are working full-time in real estate, as interesting as it is, you may wonder what the point of leaving your job was. Certainly, if you were miserable at your job, that is another matter—but having the freedom to engage in the activities that you love while collecting passive income represents a different lifestyle than the person who is hard at work flipping properties or managing workers on site.

Funding Your Purchase

There are several ways to fund your real estate investment. Many people choose to go with the tried and true method and get a conventional mortgage, but there are other options. Some options, such as FHA loans and some other government programs, may not be feasible for some real estate investors as they generally require the buyer to live on the property. That being said, there are many options available to you.

- Conventional Mortgages

- Cash-only Purchases

- Partnerships

- Home Equity Loans

- Owner-financed Purchases

- Commercial Loans

At this point, you have an idea of how conventional mortgages work. You find a mortgage lender (such as a bank), and they finance your mortgage with some money down from you. One of the great things about mortgages is that the rent that you collect may cover the entirety of your mortgage payments. The idea is that (hopefully) you will have some cash left over. Cash-only purchases avoid some of the risk associated with mortgages as the question of whether or not you will be able to make the mortgage payment is moot as you have no monthly payment to make.

In a partnership, you share the cost of the purchase with the partner. In fact, the arrangement that you have with the partner is entirely up to the partner and you. Perhaps the partner will pay all of the up-front costs for the property while you take on other responsibilities of value like repair, maintenance, etc. In a partnership, it is important to have a clear agreement so that everyone knows what is expected on their end and there is no risk of confusion later on.

Home equity loans will be familiar to most people. You gain equity in your home by making mortgage payments. Equity can also be gained by appreciation in the value of your home. You can use this equity to fund the purchase of a new property. Indeed, this is a popular way to use existing properties to acquire more, thereby building a portfolio of properties. Even if you do not use this for your first purchase, you can keep it in mind for future purchases.

Owner-financed purchases involve an agreement between the owner and the purchaser that circumvents the bank entirely. In other words, you agree to purchase the property directly from the owner, usually in the form of a monthly payment, without having a mortgage. The drawback here is that the owner may at a future date ask for the entirety of the outstanding balance of the property. In spite of this, owner-financed options have been in use for a long time and those who opt for this infrequently run into problems.

Commercial loans are almost another can of worms because these are loans specifically for commercial properties. There is not a world of difference between commercial loans and residential loans or mortgages. Commercial loans tend to have higher interest rates. They also tend to be loaned for greater amounts, as they are frequently larger properties. If you are planning in investing in commercial property, a commercial loan may be the route you end up taking.

As a last final word on real estate investing for passive income, it is important to make the point that time is money. One of the great things about generating passive income through real estate is that you are able to use your time for other things. You may choose to travel, or you may choose to spend your time with your family—you can do whatever you want with your time! A project that represents a large investment in your time may not be a good investment, especially if the return is minimal. Hence, keep that in mind. Your time has value, and that's something that every investor should remember.

Chapter 3: Using Real Estate as a Form of Passive Income

Non-traditional revenue streams are a major trend in the American economy. Although much of this change has to do with the internet and ways that men and women are able to generate revenue using internet marketing and social media, individuals in other areas have also been able to take advantage of this trend. For many people, this means increasing their potential income. Working a full-time job while also having a revenue stream from a passive source is a great way to maximize your time and increase your net worth.

In this chapter, we hope to convince you that you can successfully generate passive income through real estate investing. It is not difficult. The important thing for you to do is to have realistic expectations about what you can earn through real estate investing and how much you need to survive. In reality, everyone's situation is different. Some men and women are reading this on their own homes outright and do not have to be concerned with mortgage payments. That means that their monthly expenses are low.

However, being able to meet their monthly obligations is not so easy and not a legitimate concern for most people. Most Americans have mortgage payments or monthly rent, insurance payments, telephone and utility expenses, credit card payments, transportation costs, and other expenses. If you are like most Americans, you need to be fully prepared to enter real estate investing as a source of passive income because you need to make sure that you are able to meet your monthly obligations.

This does not mean that passive income is not for you. Passive income is for everyone. As we have already noted, passive income and other non-traditional forms of income is the direction that the economy is moving in. This means that you will have to adapt to keep pace with everyone else. People who do not adapt to their circumstances do fail—and no one wants you to fail. Understanding how passive income works and how to make it work for you is one of the important goals of this book—and it is *not* hard.

Why Is Thinking About Passive Income a Good Idea?

As we stressed in the last chapter, time is money. If you are able to find a revenue stream that allows you to free up your time, you have the potential to devote that time to other pursuits—be they pursuits that lead to more income or otherwise. Some people use passive sources of income, like real estate investing, to go back to school. If you do not have to spend your time working, then you can have more time for education. If you are lucky and plan well enough, you may even be able to pay for your education and other expenses with the money you have generated passively.

True financial freedom comes from being freed from the constraints of a nine-to-five job. Honoré de Balzac pondered that in a society based primarily around commerce, as the one that we live in is, freedom can only come from having finances strong enough to permit you to have what you wish and do what you wish. If you want the house of your dreams, the spouse of your dreams, and the life of your dreams— then you need to have a solid financial situation. You need to have a capital or, at the very least, a steady stream of income. This is how freedom is gained in modern societies.

Although the case can be made that a full-time job can offer you the freedom you wish, by potentially giving you a high income from salary or wages, most of the highest earners in the United States do not derive most of their net worth from salary and wages. Take a glance at the Forbes billionaire list. Try to find a billionaire whose net worth is derived primarily from wages. You won't be able to find one. Why? It's because the highest earners around the world derive their wealth primarily from assets. This can be stocks, bonds, or other properties that generate revenue like land, buildings, and other real estate properties.

Real estate is an asset that can be used to generate passive income for you and your family. Indeed, as we are attempting to stress in this chapter, you will not become wealthy solely by earning wages. A salary may give you the capital that you need to invest in an asset, but a salary will not be enough to make you wealthy or to give you true financial freedom. A smart person takes the capital that they have earned through salary and invests it into an asset. You have the choice of what type of asset to invest in. Most people reading this have considered stocks, bonds, the currency trading market, bitcoin, commodities, and the like. In this book, we hope to convince you that real estate investing is the way to go.

Why is real estate investing a better investment than other options like stocks, bitcoin, commodities, and the like? The key here is the potential for passive income. Although the aforementioned assets do contribute to your net worth on paper, in order to achieve true financial freedom, you also want to have a steady income stream to allow you to meet the demands that you likely have to meet *every* month. Real estate investing poises you to meet those needs better than any other investment, as revenue is easily and consistently collected in the form of rent every month.

The potential to be able to have a high flow of income every month is great with real estate investing. It all depends on the type of property that you invest in. Many of you will be considering the residential real estate route. That's fine. We have to mention that a commercial real estate is an option as well, although it is a little different from residential real estate investing as we mentioned in the last chapter. Again, you have other options to consider for your investment, including REITs, forming a partnership—the list goes on.

So what does this all have to do with passive income? Aside from the fact that passive income is the only true way to achieve financial freedom, real estate investing also places you at an advantage compared to others having a go at passive income streams because your real estate properties will appreciate over time. This means that you have the potential of even greater passive income as the years go on. When you invest in real estate, you not only have an asset that contributes to your net worth, but you also have steady revenue from an appreciating source. That means an appreciating return—and who doesn't want that?

So there are a number of reasons why you should consider passive income. For one thing, passive income is the trend of the future, and you do not want to be left behind. On top of that, passive income is the only way to achieve true financial freedom—freedom from the toil of a nine-to-five and the daily concerns of money. Finally, passive income derived from real estate properties, in particular, can protect you from the rising unemployment rate, economic downturns, and all of the other things that can ruin the chance of achieving financial freedom.

Real Estate Investing Can Be Done with a Minimal Time Commitment

Most of the time, commitment to real estate investing comes in the beginning. Assessing your financial situation to determine what you can afford, figuring out what your monthly expenses are (especially if you are considering leaving your job), scouting the national real estate market (or local, depending on how you choose to approach this) to figure out what your options are for investment, going to the bank and getting a pre-approval letter, educating yourself on real estate investment trusts, and looking for a partner—all of the heavy lifting with real estate investing comes in the beginning.

Once you have handled all the preliminary things, which will be discussed in more detail in the next two chapters, you are ready to purchase your property. Once you have your property, you are ready to rent, assuming that there are no major repairs or refurbishes needed—and once you are renting, the hard work has already been done. You now have passive income from a source that you have devoted your time and money into. At that point, the time required is minimal.

You will have to check on your property and keep in communication with tenants. You will also have to make sure that any bills or taxes that you are responsible for are paid, but this is a much lower commitment in terms of time than most people have at a nine-to-five job. Now that you have your real estate investment property, you will find that you have time to do whatever you want and that there is no price that can be placed on that type of freedom.

Chapter 4: Leaving Your Job and Obtaining Financial Freedom

One of the goals of this book is to prepare you to obtain the *true* financial freedom that comes from deriving your income passively from real estate. There are many ways to do this, but the dream of many people is to be able to leave their full-time employment and obtain their income primarily from passive sources—in this case, real estate investing. As we have touched on in other chapters, it is certainly possible to have a full-time job at the same time as you are obtaining your income passively from real estate. That is something for you to keep in mind. The choice of which setup is right for you is entirely up to you.

In this chapter, we hope to expose you to how you can quit your job and devote yourself to earning income passively. The purpose of this chapter is to give you an idea of what you need to do before you leave your job. The last thing you want to do is quit your job and find that your financial situation wasn't as strong as you previously thought it was. It will be very important for you that you are able to have a clear understanding of your resources, your obligations, and your overall financial situation before you leave your job.

Lay Out Your Financial Situation Clearly

Perhaps the most important thing for you to do if you are considering leaving your job is to devote time to very clearly laying out your financial situation. This does not mean merely the obvious of knowing how much you have in the bank, what your assets are worth, etc. You want to have a crystal clear understanding of what your monthly obligations are. This may seem obvious, but many people discover too late that their monthly outlays are more than what they previously realized. This can put you in the situation of finding out after you have already left your job that you're not able to do that. That is the last thing you want.

You want to make a list of what your assets are, including the money you have in the bank, any investments that you already have, retirement accounts, and even your car. Very clearly lay out what your assets are. The idea here is to get a sense of what you are worth right now in monetary terms. If you need to work with an accountant to do this, then you can certainly do so. Most people going into real estate investing for the first time are able to undertake this process without the help of an accountant. Indeed, it is probably a good idea to make this attempt alone, as much of this whole process of real estate investing necessitates that you take the driver's seat.

Once you have a list of your assets with monetary values, try to get a sense of what your monthly expenses are. List everything: from rent or mortgage payments to any bills that you pay regularly. Keep in mind that some bills may not be charged monthly. Maybe you have water bills or taxes that come quarterly or once a year. Don't forget about any payments that automatically debit to your checking account. These bills don't go away with a change of career. They are still going to be there, so keep a handle on them.

Next, get a sense of what new expenses you may have. If you are leaving your job, maybe you will be paying for your own health insurance, life insurance, travel expenses, and the like. Many people forget about these, and it is important not to. Although most people are able to find affordable insurance options that do not overtax their bank account, this is still an expense that you will regularly be paying probably for the rest of your life, so it is a good idea not to forget about it.

Don't forget to think about expenses that you have that may be hard to calculate: food, clothes, other consumer items. For some people, it may be easy to calculate how much they spend a month on food, clothes, and other consumer goods, but for some others, it may be difficult. This may be a good opportunity for you to really get a handle on your finances. Are you spending too much on food? Clothes? Do you really need two cars?

The next step is kind of a holistic one. Look at the three lists that you have. You should have a list of your assets, a list of your monthly bills, an estimate of your monthly food and clothing costs, and a list of any new expenses that you will have if you quit your job. You have to make sure that once you leave your job that you will be able to meet the expenses represented by the last three lists with the assets that you have (and any revenue). Are you starting to get the picture? Leaving your job may turn out to be a lot more expensive than you thought.

If you are in the situation where you already own the property that you live in, then you are ahead of the game. Some of you out there may be financial wizards that have already invested the time and energy into keeping their expenses at an absolute minimum. If you are one of these people, then you are one step ahead of the game. The goal of this exercise is to make sure that you fully understand your financial situation, but it's also to help you perhaps take a closer look at areas where you might be spending too much.

Let's go over the steps to take to establish your financial picture fully.

- Make a list of current assets.

- Make a list of current sources of revenue.

- Make a list of monthly bills (like rent, taxes, insurance, and car payments).

- Make an estimate of monthly expenses (like food).

- Make an estimate of new expenses that you may have if you quit your job.

Equipped with this knowledge, you may decide that you are not ready to leave your job right now. You may decide that you do not want to leave full-time employment at all. Perhaps the best option for you is to invest in the real estate industry while working full-time in something else. There is nothing wrong with that. Lots of people do it. This process should help you get an idea of what is realistic for you, and leaving your job may not be a realistic option right now.

Leaving Your Job and Becoming Self-Employed

Some of you will decide that you are ready to leave your job. Maybe not now, but soon. You have enough assets and savings to cover any gaps in income. Maybe you have decided that you will invest in real estate and once you start earning passive income that way, then you will quit your job. What's fun about real estate investing is that you are constantly faced with choices. You choose what's best for you and your economic situation.

Now that you have an idea of your financial picture and what you are able to handle realistically in terms of income, you now are ready to go through the steps of actually leaving your job. No, do not walk up to your boss and say "I quit," slam the door, and walk out. One of the most important concepts in business is that maintaining good relationships with people is crucial. You never know. You may not to walk back into that job one day and deal with that boss that you slammed the door on. Maybe your boss's sister or wife is a figure in the local real estate community or on the commerce board. Always maintain good relationships with others because you just never know who knows who and who you might meet again.

What's the point? The point is that there is some unpredictability in life. Everyone experiences drawbacks. Everyone experiences ups and downs. Even if you are sure that you are ready to leave your job, you still want to do it the right way.

How do you leave your job the right way? Well, it is not too hard. Leaving aside cases of emergencies or extremely dire situations, you want to do this face-to-face. Set up a time to meet. When you do meet your boss, you don't have to tell him or her everything, but you can essentially say that you are planning a career change and you are therefore giving your notice. The general rule is to give at least two weeks, but this will vary on the industry. In some industries, you may be expected to give a month's notice or more. Your boss may want to know what you are doing after you leave. It is up to you how much you reveal. If you choose to divulge your forays into real estate, it is possible that your boss may have some advice or want to help.

Concerns After You Leave Your Job

The big things after you leave your current career, aside from the obvious one of making sure you actually have the money you need to meet your obligations, involve preparing yourself for your new career and the ins and out of being in business for yourself. We do not live in ancient times in which you might have a business and really not have to worry too much about the tax man, keeping records, auditing, and the like. We live in the United States in the 21st century, so if you are going into business for yourself, you need to make sure that you are ready for that.

So what are some of the concerns that you should think about before setting up shop as a real estate investor:

- Should you go into business for yourself or should you look for a partner?

- Are you going to purchase a rental property or invest in a REIT or other type of asset?

- How should you structure your business: LLC, sole proprietorship, corporation?

- Tax issues

The reality is that everyone's situation is different. Perhaps you already are familiar with the financial industry, and perhaps you know that you want an LLC and you already have a friend who is going to handle the tax side of things for you. If that is your situation, then you are one step ahead of the game. However, for everyone else, these are things that you need to think about. Sure, you may already have the money, but are you ready for the business side of things?

In the next chapter, we will take all that we have learned from the last three chapters to take you step by step through the process of working a nine-to-five like most Americans and becoming a real estate investor with a steady stream of passive income. It is not as difficult as you think, and you may be surprised by how much knowledge you have already gained.

Chapter 5: How-to Guide of Real Estate Investing

Like it or not, this is a process that you need to take step by step. Sure, you can dive in head-first if you want. You might be tempted to do so if you have a nice bundle of cash in the bank waiting for you to invest. Even if that is the case, the people with the best outcomes are those who take each step carefully, making sure they fully understand what they are doing at each point in the process. In this chapter, we hope to summarize all that you have learned in order to walk you through the process.

First things first, the real estate market is not as bad as you think. These are the current characteristics of the American real estate market in 2019:

- Increasing interest rates from the Fed

- An overall reduction in new housing construction compared to prior decades

- A general lack of supply of affordable housing

- Changing economic patterns impacting home buying trends

- A glut of renters on the market

The takeaway point here is that the real estate market is not something that you should be scared of. You are ready to invest—you just need to make sure that you make a good investment. A good investment should appreciate and have a good rate of return. That means that the property should increase in value, and the amount of revenue that you derive from the property per year should be a good percentage of what you invested (5% or 6% is considered good). This assures that the automatic revenue that you get from rent represents a fair amount back based on your investment.

After understanding the real estate market, you have some decisions to make. What kind of real estate investment do you want to make? Here are some of your options:

- Purchase a rental property.

- Purchase and resell property (flipping).

- Rent a space in a property that you already own.

- Invest in a real estate project.

- Invest in a real estate investment trust or REIT.

There are many ways that you can use your money, and you have to figure out which best suits your needs, your finances, and your goals.

Once you have a sense of how you might go about investing in the market, you have to figure out if you truly want to devote yourself to earning income passively or if you want to maintain a full-time job. If you do plan to leave your full-time employment, here are some things to do first.

- Make a list of current assets.

- Make a list of current sources of revenue.

- Make a list of monthly bills and expenses.

- Make an estimate of new expenses that may result after you leave your job (like insurance).

Finally, you will be going into business for yourself, so you need to make sure that you are set-up and ready-to-go. Here are some things that you should think about:

- Choosing between a sole proprietorship, LLC, corporation, or partnership;

- Working from home or renting an office;

- Keeping good records for tax purposes and follow the law to the letter; and

- Opening up a business account at the bank.

Frequently Asked Questions

1. What makes real estate such a good investment?

    Real estate is regarded by many people as one of the best investments that you can make with your money. People have been investing their money in what we call real estate for as long as there has been private property and laws to protect them. Real estate is regarded as such a good investment because the value of real estate naturally increases over time due to various factors like the increase in GDP, inflation, currency exchange, and economic expansion—all of which are related to one another in some degree.

    Because the value of real estate naturally increases over time (generally), the real estate investor is presented with the possibility of drastically increasing their income and their net worth merely by holding on to property. You can compound this favorable financial situation by acquiring more property—leading to miraculous financial growth in a relatively short span of time. Few other investments can promise the same, leaving real estate as arguably the best investment that you can make.

2. Do I have enough money to enter the real estate market?

    Anyone with capital on hand can invest in the real estate market. Because there are many different types of properties that you can invest in and because the market in the United States is so large, you do not need a specific amount of capital or money to enter the market. Also, there are various ways that you can raise capital without having cash on hand. Equity in a house or other form of property can be used to acquire real estate. This is a technique that you can use not only to acquire your first property but also to acquire additional properties after you've made your first acquisition.

3. What do I need to know about interest rates?

It is important to have some knowledge about interest rates. Interest rates are set by the Federal government, and they impact the mortgage rates that will be available to you when investing in property. Interest rates also impact the general picture of the real estate market. Higher interest rates can discourage potential homebuyers and other real estate investors from investing in property.

What a higher interest rate means to you as a real estate investor is not entirely straightforward. Yes, a higher interest rate means that you may have to pay back a loan at a slightly higher rate than previously, but it also means that the market for renters might be larger than it might otherwise be. From your standpoint, this is good, as you will be renting the properties that you acquire to renters. Interest rates can also indirectly impact the values of real estate, especially increases over time, but careful investing can mitigate some of these risks.

4. Is the market slowing?

This is a big question that many people are asking right now. Concerns about the market slowing is a topic of concern for many people because a slowing market may indicate that housing values will no longer increase at rates that they'd had in the past. Housing values may even fall if the market in a particular area is overvalued, as happened in some parts of the country after the real estate bubble burst 15 years ago.

What you need to know here is that there is a debate about whether the market will slow in 2019 or in the years to come. Even when the market has slowed or experienced downturns in the past, people were still able to engage in real estate investing successfully. Indeed, some people believe that it is better to invest when prices are flattening than when they are continuing a dramatic rise. In short, even if the market does show signs of slowing in some areas, there are definitely parts of the country that are undervalued in terms of their real estate— representing perfect opportunities for the opportunistic buyer to enter the market.

5. What's the difference between real estate investing for passive income versus real estate investing in general?

There is a fine line between real estate investing full-time and real estate investing for passive income. What we mean by that is both endeavors do involve an investment of time and money on your part. The difference is that some people choose to devote their time in the day to scouting for property and increasing the value of their real estate portfolio by continuously looking for opportunities to invest.

The real estate investor looking to the industry primarily as a source of passive income will make an initial investment of time and money and then let their investment do the rest. As a real estate investor, you do not have to devote a significant period of time in the day to continue to scout the market if you do not want to. A real estate investor with a large portfolio of properties—one who is actively managing properties and looking for new investment opportunities—straddles the line between passive income and full-time income.

6. Are there any IRS concerns that I should have if my primary income is from real estate investing?

The IRS is known to become curious when they see that an individual filing their taxes has steady income without full-time employment. Of course, this situation applies to many investors, and there is no illegality that's necessarily evident in this case. Some people choose to have some form of full-time employment in order to give the appearance of "working" to the IRS. The reality is that the real estate investor does not have to do this.

Working with an accountant throughout the year or at tax filing time is an easy way to avoid any tax worries. Also, if your real estate investing is set up in the form of a business in which you are the proprietor, it can be construed as full-time employment—just one that in reality gives you a lot of free time. See the difference? In the case of a real estate investor, the difference between full-time employment and part-time employment is really just semantics.

7. Can I really achieve financial freedom through investing in real estate?

Countless Americans have achieved financial freedom by investing in real estate. Indeed, more people have likely become millionaires through real estate than through any other means. Yes, you can achieve financial freedom through real estate, but this does involve some work on your part. Much of the work that is required from you is in the realm of education.

Individuals can make good investments, and they can make bad investments—and this is just as true of real estate investing as it is of the stock market, currency trading, commodities, or any other form of investing.

One of your goals in reading this book is knowing the difference between a good investment and a bad investment. There are unfortunately bad investments in real estate, and your goal is to avoid those as much as possible. A bad investment is a waste of time and money. It will steer you away from your goal of achieving financial freedom through investing. True, we all have slips and falls, which may mean making the occasional bad investment—but the trick is to learn enough about the trade to avoid making those.

8. How much money do I need to get started?

There is no definite amount of money that you need to get started, primarily because there are many different types of properties selling at different values. You also have the choice of how much to pay down and how long of a mortgage you would like to take. As detailed in this book, it is generally a good idea not to invest all of your savings in the market. This will provide you with a little bit of a buffer in case of emergencies or unexpected expenses.

9. What type of property should I invest in?

Many of you reading this are planning to invest in residential real estate, and this book assumes that this is the form of real estate that you will be investing in because it has the potential to reward you the quickest. There is also commercial real estate, which often involves a larger investment in time and capital, not to mention that the payout is frequently longer term. There is nothing stopping you from achieving your financial freedom through a commercial estate, although this book assumes that you will be going the more common route of investing with residential real estate, which provides a quick and steady payout through the collection of rent.

10. When is a good time to start investing in more property?

This is really the million-dollar question. Investing in real estate can be so enjoyable and rewarding to the point that it becomes addictive to people. The analogy to gambling is clear here, as there is a risk that comes with investing in real estate just as there is in playing a hand at the blackjack table or roulette. You will have to make a decision for yourself about when the right time is to invest in more property. This decision will be based on your own financial picture, how well you are doing with your first property, and the state of the market.

Conclusion

Congratulations on reaching the end of *Real Estate Investing for Passive Income*. Here, you were introduced to the concepts that will allow you to achieve your dream of achieving financial freedom through real estate investing. Real estate poses an incredible opportunity for the investor who is willing to invest time into learning the industry inside and out. Learning the industry allows you to do what thousands before you have done—sit back and enjoy the passive income that comes with making the right investment.

Naturally, the question on the minds of many people is: "Where is the industry going, and what can we expect in the future?" Although concerns about general economic cooling are not without merit, the real estate industry is still vibrant, representing an excellent opportunity for an investor looking to make a solid investment. Unemployment rates are low in the United States, but ups and downs in the stock market, as well as concerns about changes in the face of the American workplace, have muddied the overall economic picture in the country. The economy is still strong, and questions about interest rate will impact what the real estate picture looks like in the future.

What this means for you as a new investor in real estate looking to generate passive income is that *now* is as good a time as any to invest in the market. One concept that we have tried to hammer home in this book is that there is a difference between a good investment and a bad investment. A good investment is one in which all indicators suggest that the value of properties in the area of purchase has been rising steadily and gives the picture that values will continue to rise. Some markets are clearly overpriced, and purchasing a property that is overpriced or unnaturally inflated is not a good investment.

In the first chapter, we hoped to help you understand the distinction between a good investment and a bad investment by detailing the current real estate picture in the United States. In order to understand the current real estate picture, it is important to get a sense of where the nation has been since the last industry slump 15 years ago, which was part of a global trend that was actually more dramatic in other countries. Understanding the current picture and the possibility of a flattening in the market should help you make the right sort of risk—a risk that will lead to a solid payout.

The reality is that you will be investing your money in this market, so you do want to make sure that you are not investing in overpriced properties or parts of the country that are more likely to be impacted in an economic slump.

In the second chapter, we prepared you for your real estate journey by introducing you to some of the concepts that you will need to be familiar with in order to have a successful foray into real estate. This will be a learning experience for you, so learning some of the important concepts is a good first step to get you on your way.

In the third chapter, we delved more deeply into passive income to help you understand what your life will be like as a real estate investor with a lot of free time on your hands. A point that we drove home in this book is that you can invest as much or as little time in this adventure as you would like. Some people choose to invest more time, and with that often comes a bigger financial investment. Anyone with a real estate property that is accruing rental income is able to have some free time because of this passive income source, although some investors choose to invest this back into their businesses. Remember that your time is a form of financial investment. As the saying goes, time *is* money.

Presumably, your goal is to eventually leave your full-time employment in order to begin the odyssey of investing your time and money into real estate. In the fourth chapter, we explained the ins and outs of leaving your job and some of the things that you need to keep in mind before doing so. Some of these concerns are issues of making sure that you have enough savings, setting up health and life insurance, and tax issues that come along with being self-employed. We also addressed the issue of whether you should go through it alone or consider partnering up.

Prepared with all of the tools you need to understand the real estate market and embark on your journey, we broke down the whole process step by step in the fifth chapter. The goal here was to make the process as straightforward as possible for you so that you can quickly and efficiently go from working full-time to transitioning to living your dream by generating passive income through real estate. Many Americans are able to live their dreams of travel, time with family, or whatever it is that they desire through real estate —and the goal of this chapter was to make this process as simple as possible for you.

You are now ready to embark on your journey, but it is important to remember that there is some ongoing learning that is a part of this process. This is true to any endeavor, but it is especially true to real estate, as this market can change very quickly due to economic and governmental factors. It is a good idea to get into the habit of keeping up-to-date on trends in the market in order to make the most of your investment. The point here is to be prepared for whatever comes in an industry that can change very quickly.

However, the reality is that there will always be some value in real estate, unlike other markets like stocks or bitcoin that can lose most of their value very quickly. There will always be some value in your property, and the right rental property will continue to provide a source of income for you far into the future. Now, you know what you need in order to make the most out of your foray into real estate investing. We wish you the best of luck, and we know that it is only a matter of time before you achieve everything that you set out to achieve.

www.ingramcontent.com/pod-product-compliance
Lightning Source LLC
Chambersburg PA
CBHW072259170526
45158CB00003BA/1113